Parent Teacher Communication Log

Year at a glance

August	**September**	**October**
November	**December**	**January**
February	**March**	**April**
May	**June**	**July**

Student Name	
Parents Name	
Address	
Phone Number	Home: Work:
Email	

Date	
Person Contacted	
Method Of Contact	
Reason	
Notes	

Date	
Person Contacted	
Method Of Contact	
Reason	
Notes	

Date	
Person Contacted	
Method Of Contact	
Reason	

Notes

Date	
Person Contacted	
Method Of Contact	
Reason	

Notes

Date	
Person Contacted	
Method Of Contact	
Reason	

Notes

Student Name	
Parents Name	
Address	
Phone Number	Home: Work:
Email	

Date	
Person Contacted	
Method Of Contact	
Reason	
Notes	

Date	
Person Contacted	
Method Of Contact	
Reason	
Notes	

Date	
Person Contacted	
Method Of Contact	
Reason	

Notes

Date	
Person Contacted	
Method Of Contact	
Reason	

Notes

Date	
Person Contacted	
Method Of Contact	
Reason	

Notes

Student Name	
Parents Name	
Address	
Phone Number	Home: Work:
Email	

Date	
Person Contacted	
Method Of Contact	
Reason	
Notes	

Date	
Person Contacted	
Method Of Contact	
Reason	
Notes	

Date	
Person Contacted	
Method Of Contact	
Reason	
Notes	

Date	
Person Contacted	
Method Of Contact	
Reason	
Notes	

Date	
Person Contacted	
Method Of Contact	
Reason	
Notes	

Student Name	
Parents Name	
Address	
Phone Number	Home: Work:
Email	

Date	
Person Contacted	
Method Of Contact	
Reason	
Notes	

Date	
Person Contacted	
Method Of Contact	
Reason	
Notes	

Date	
Person Contacted	
Method Of Contact	
Reason	

Notes

Date	
Person Contacted	
Method Of Contact	
Reason	

Notes

Date	
Person Contacted	
Method Of Contact	
Reason	

Notes

Student Name	
Parents Name	
Address	
Phone Number	Home: Work:
Email	

Date	
Person Contacted	
Method Of Contact	
Reason	
Notes	

Date	
Person Contacted	
Method Of Contact	
Reason	
Notes	

Date	
Person Contacted	
Method Of Contact	
Reason	

Notes

Date	
Person Contacted	
Method Of Contact	
Reason	

Notes

Date	
Person Contacted	
Method Of Contact	
Reason	

Notes

Student Name	
Parents Name	
Address	
Phone Number	Home: Work:
Email	

Date	
Person Contacted	
Method Of Contact	
Reason	
Notes	

Date	
Person Contacted	
Method Of Contact	
Reason	
Notes	

Date	
Person Contacted	
Method Of Contact	
Reason	

Notes

Date	
Person Contacted	
Method Of Contact	
Reason	

Notes

Date	
Person Contacted	
Method Of Contact	
Reason	

Notes

Student Name	
Parents Name	
Address	
Phone Number	Home: Work:
Email	

Date	
Person Contacted	
Method Of Contact	
Reason	

Notes

Date	
Person Contacted	
Method Of Contact	
Reason	

Notes

Date	
Person Contacted	
Method Of Contact	
Reason	
Notes	

Date	
Person Contacted	
Method Of Contact	
Reason	
Notes	

Date	
Person Contacted	
Method Of Contact	
Reason	
Notes	

Student Name	
Parents Name	
Address	
Phone Number	Home: Work:
Email	

Date	
Person Contacted	
Method Of Contact	
Reason	
Notes	

Date	
Person Contacted	
Method Of Contact	
Reason	
Notes	

Date	
Person Contacted	
Method Of Contact	
Reason	

Notes

Date	
Person Contacted	
Method Of Contact	
Reason	

Notes

Date	
Person Contacted	
Method Of Contact	
Reason	

Notes

Student Name	
Parents Name	
Address	
Phone Number	Home: Work:
Email	

Date	
Person Contacted	
Method Of Contact	
Reason	
Notes	

Date	
Person Contacted	
Method Of Contact	
Reason	
Notes	

Date	
Person Contacted	
Method Of Contact	
Reason	
Notes	

Date	
Person Contacted	
Method Of Contact	
Reason	
Notes	

Date	
Person Contacted	
Method Of Contact	
Reason	
Notes	

Student Name	
Parents Name	
Address	
Phone Number	Home: Work:
Email	

Date	
Person Contacted	
Method Of Contact	
Reason	
Notes	

Date	
Person Contacted	
Method Of Contact	
Reason	
Notes	

Date	
Person Contacted	
Method Of Contact	
Reason	

Notes

Date	
Person Contacted	
Method Of Contact	
Reason	

Notes

Date	
Person Contacted	
Method Of Contact	
Reason	

Notes

Student Name	
Parents Name	
Address	
Phone Number	Home: Work:
Email	

Date	
Person Contacted	
Method Of Contact	
Reason	
Notes	

Date	
Person Contacted	
Method Of Contact	
Reason	
Notes	

Date	
Person Contacted	
Method Of Contact	
Reason	

Notes

Date	
Person Contacted	
Method Of Contact	
Reason	

Notes

Date	
Person Contacted	
Method Of Contact	
Reason	

Notes

Student Name	
Parents Name	
Address	
Phone Number	Home: Work:
Email	

Date	
Person Contacted	
Method Of Contact	
Reason	
Notes	

Date	
Person Contacted	
Method Of Contact	
Reason	
Notes	

Date	
Person Contacted	
Method Of Contact	
Reason	

Notes

Date	
Person Contacted	
Method Of Contact	
Reason	

Notes

Date	
Person Contacted	
Method Of Contact	
Reason	

Notes

Student Name	
Parents Name	
Address	
Phone Number	Home: Work:
Email	

Date	
Person Contacted	
Method Of Contact	
Reason	

Notes

Date	
Person Contacted	
Method Of Contact	
Reason	

Notes

Date	
Person Contacted	
Method Of Contact	
Reason	
Notes	

Date	
Person Contacted	
Method Of Contact	
Reason	
Notes	

Date	
Person Contacted	
Method Of Contact	
Reason	
Notes	

Student Name	
Parents Name	
Address	
Phone Number	Home: Work:
Email	

Date	
Person Contacted	
Method Of Contact	
Reason	
Notes	

Date	
Person Contacted	
Method Of Contact	
Reason	
Notes	

Date	
Person Contacted	
Method Of Contact	
Reason	

Notes

Date	
Person Contacted	
Method Of Contact	
Reason	

Notes

Date	
Person Contacted	
Method Of Contact	
Reason	

Notes

Student Name	
Parents Name	
Address	
Phone Number	Home: Work:
Email	

Date	
Person Contacted	
Method Of Contact	
Reason	
Notes	

Date	
Person Contacted	
Method Of Contact	
Reason	
Notes	

Date	
Person Contacted	
Method Of Contact	
Reason	
Notes	

Date	
Person Contacted	
Method Of Contact	
Reason	
Notes	

Date	
Person Contacted	
Method Of Contact	
Reason	
Notes	

Student Name	
Parents Name	
Address	
Phone Number	Home: Work:
Email	

Date	
Person Contacted	
Method Of Contact	
Reason	
Notes	

Date	
Person Contacted	
Method Of Contact	
Reason	
Notes	

Date	
Person Contacted	
Method Of Contact	
Reason	

Notes

Date	
Person Contacted	
Method Of Contact	
Reason	

Notes

Date	
Person Contacted	
Method Of Contact	
Reason	

Notes

Student Name	
Parents Name	
Address	
Phone Number	Home: Work:
Email	

Date	
Person Contacted	
Method Of Contact	
Reason	

Notes

Date	
Person Contacted	
Method Of Contact	
Reason	

Notes

Date	
Person Contacted	
Method Of Contact	
Reason	
Notes	

Date	
Person Contacted	
Method Of Contact	
Reason	
Notes	

Date	
Person Contacted	
Method Of Contact	
Reason	
Notes	

Student Name	
Parents Name	
Address	
Phone Number	Home: Work:
Email	

Date	
Person Contacted	
Method Of Contact	
Reason	
Notes	

Date	
Person Contacted	
Method Of Contact	
Reason	
Notes	

Date	
Person Contacted	
Method Of Contact	
Reason	

Notes

Date	
Person Contacted	
Method Of Contact	
Reason	

Notes

Date	
Person Contacted	
Method Of Contact	
Reason	

Notes

Student Name	
Parents Name	
Address	
Phone Number	Home: Work:
Email	

Date	
Person Contacted	
Method Of Contact	
Reason	

Notes

Date	
Person Contacted	
Method Of Contact	
Reason	

Notes

Date	
Person Contacted	
Method Of Contact	
Reason	
Notes	

Date	
Person Contacted	
Method Of Contact	
Reason	
Notes	

Date	
Person Contacted	
Method Of Contact	
Reason	
Notes	

Student Name	
Parents Name	
Address	
Phone Number	Home: Work:
Email	

Date	
Person Contacted	
Method Of Contact	
Reason	
Notes	

Date	
Person Contacted	
Method Of Contact	
Reason	
Notes	

Date	
Person Contacted	
Method Of Contact	
Reason	
Notes	

Date	
Person Contacted	
Method Of Contact	
Reason	
Notes	

Date	
Person Contacted	
Method Of Contact	
Reason	
Notes	

Student Name	
Parents Name	
Address	
Phone Number	Home: Work:
Email	

Date	
Person Contacted	
Method Of Contact	
Reason	
Notes	

Date	
Person Contacted	
Method Of Contact	
Reason	
Notes	

Date	
Person Contacted	
Method Of Contact	
Reason	
Notes	

Date	
Person Contacted	
Method Of Contact	
Reason	
Notes	

Date	
Person Contacted	
Method Of Contact	
Reason	
Notes	

Student Name	
Parents Name	
Address	
Phone Number	Home: Work:
Email	

Date	
Person Contacted	
Method Of Contact	
Reason	
Notes	

Date	
Person Contacted	
Method Of Contact	
Reason	
Notes	

Date	
Person Contacted	
Method Of Contact	
Reason	
Notes	

Date	
Person Contacted	
Method Of Contact	
Reason	
Notes	

Date	
Person Contacted	
Method Of Contact	
Reason	
Notes	

Student Name	
Parents Name	
Address	
Phone Number	Home: Work:
Email	

Date	
Person Contacted	
Method Of Contact	
Reason	
Notes	

Date	
Person Contacted	
Method Of Contact	
Reason	
Notes	

Date	
Person Contacted	
Method Of Contact	
Reason	

Notes

Date	
Person Contacted	
Method Of Contact	
Reason	

Notes

Date	
Person Contacted	
Method Of Contact	
Reason	

Notes

Student Name	
Parents Name	
Address	
Phone Number	Home: Work:
Email	

Date	
Person Contacted	
Method Of Contact	
Reason	
Notes	

Date	
Person Contacted	
Method Of Contact	
Reason	
Notes	

Date	
Person Contacted	
Method Of Contact	
Reason	

Notes

Date	
Person Contacted	
Method Of Contact	
Reason	

Notes

Date	
Person Contacted	
Method Of Contact	
Reason	

Notes

Student Name	
Parents Name	
Address	
Phone Number	Home: Work:
Email	

Date	
Person Contacted	
Method Of Contact	
Reason	
Notes	

Date	
Person Contacted	
Method Of Contact	
Reason	
Notes	

Date	
Person Contacted	
Method Of Contact	
Reason	
Notes	

Date	
Person Contacted	
Method Of Contact	
Reason	
Notes	

Date	
Person Contacted	
Method Of Contact	
Reason	
Notes	

Student Name	
Parents Name	
Address	
Phone Number	Home: Work:
Email	

Date	
Person Contacted	
Method Of Contact	
Reason	
Notes	

Date	
Person Contacted	
Method Of Contact	
Reason	
Notes	

Date	
Person Contacted	
Method Of Contact	
Reason	

Notes

Date	
Person Contacted	
Method Of Contact	
Reason	

Notes

Date	
Person Contacted	
Method Of Contact	
Reason	

Notes

Student Name	
Parents Name	
Address	
Phone Number	Home: Work:
Email	

Date	
Person Contacted	
Method Of Contact	
Reason	
Notes	

Date	
Person Contacted	
Method Of Contact	
Reason	
Notes	

Date	
Person Contacted	
Method Of Contact	
Reason	

Notes

Date	
Person Contacted	
Method Of Contact	
Reason	

Notes

Date	
Person Contacted	
Method Of Contact	
Reason	

Notes

Student Name	
Parents Name	
Address	
Phone Number	Home: Work:
Email	

Date	
Person Contacted	
Method Of Contact	
Reason	
Notes	

Date	
Person Contacted	
Method Of Contact	
Reason	
Notes	

Date	
Person Contacted	
Method Of Contact	
Reason	

Notes

Date	
Person Contacted	
Method Of Contact	
Reason	

Notes

Date	
Person Contacted	
Method Of Contact	
Reason	

Notes

Student Name	
Parents Name	
Address	
Phone Number	Home: Work:
Email	

Date	
Person Contacted	
Method Of Contact	
Reason	
Notes	

Date	
Person Contacted	
Method Of Contact	
Reason	
Notes	

Date	
Person Contacted	
Method Of Contact	
Reason	

Notes

Date	
Person Contacted	
Method Of Contact	
Reason	

Notes

Date	
Person Contacted	
Method Of Contact	
Reason	

Notes

Student Name	
Parents Name	
Address	
Phone Number	Home: Work:
Email	

Date	
Person Contacted	
Method Of Contact	
Reason	
Notes	

Date	
Person Contacted	
Method Of Contact	
Reason	
Notes	

Date	
Person Contacted	
Method Of Contact	
Reason	

Notes

Date	
Person Contacted	
Method Of Contact	
Reason	

Notes

Date	
Person Contacted	
Method Of Contact	
Reason	

Notes

Student Name	
Parents Name	
Address	
Phone Number	Home: Work:
Email	

Date	
Person Contacted	
Method Of Contact	
Reason	

Notes

Date	
Person Contacted	
Method Of Contact	
Reason	

Notes

Date	
Person Contacted	
Method Of Contact	
Reason	
Notes	

Date	
Person Contacted	
Method Of Contact	
Reason	
Notes	

Date	
Person Contacted	
Method Of Contact	
Reason	
Notes	

Student Name	
Parents Name	
Address	
Phone Number	Home: Work:
Email	

Date	
Person Contacted	
Method Of Contact	
Reason	
Notes	

Date	
Person Contacted	
Method Of Contact	
Reason	
Notes	

Date	
Person Contacted	
Method Of Contact	
Reason	
Notes	

Date	
Person Contacted	
Method Of Contact	
Reason	
Notes	

Date	
Person Contacted	
Method Of Contact	
Reason	
Notes	

Student Name	
Parents Name	
Address	
Phone Number	Home: Work:
Email	

Date	
Person Contacted	
Method Of Contact	
Reason	
Notes	

Date	
Person Contacted	
Method Of Contact	
Reason	
Notes	

Date	
Person Contacted	
Method Of Contact	
Reason	
Notes	

Date	
Person Contacted	
Method Of Contact	
Reason	
Notes	

Date	
Person Contacted	
Method Of Contact	
Reason	
Notes	

Student Name	
Parents Name	
Address	
Phone Number	Home: Work:
Email	

Date	
Person Contacted	
Method Of Contact	
Reason	
Notes	

Date	
Person Contacted	
Method Of Contact	
Reason	
Notes	

Date	
Person Contacted	
Method Of Contact	
Reason	
Notes	

Date	
Person Contacted	
Method Of Contact	
Reason	
Notes	

Date	
Person Contacted	
Method Of Contact	
Reason	
Notes	

Student Name	
Parents Name	
Address	
Phone Number	Home: Work:
Email	

Date	
Person Contacted	
Method Of Contact	
Reason	

Notes

Date	
Person Contacted	
Method Of Contact	
Reason	

Notes

Date	
Person Contacted	
Method Of Contact	
Reason	
Notes	

Date	
Person Contacted	
Method Of Contact	
Reason	
Notes	

Date	
Person Contacted	
Method Of Contact	
Reason	
Notes	

Made in United States
Orlando, FL
21 July 2022